Poems About Anger

by America's Children

edited by Jacqueline Sweeney

MARSHALL CAVENDISH
NEW YORK

For the innocent victims of misdirected anger—which is all of us.

The publisher and editor would like to thank the following schools for opening their doors to us: Alden Place and Elm Drive Elementary Schools (Millbrook Central School District), Amenia and Millerton Elementary Schools (Webutuck School District), Barnum Woods Elementary School (East Meadow Union Free School District), Beekman, LaGrange, and Noxon Road Elementary Schools (Arlington Central School District), Boght Hills and Blue Creek Elementary Schools (North Colonie Central School District), Carrie E. Tompkins Elementary School (Croton-Harmon School District), Central Avenue Elementary School (Mamaroneck Union Free School District), Gardnertown Fundamental Magnet School (Newburgh Enlarged City School District), Germantown Central School (Germantown Central School District), Hackley School, Pawling Elementary and Middle Schools (Pawling Central School District), Scotchtown Avenue School (Goshen Central School District), Tesago Elementary School (Shenendehowa Central School District)

And with thanks to the art teachers (who worked so hard and were so wonderfully supportive): Christine MacPherson, Mary Molloy, Leslie Ann Pesetzky, Carole Pugliese, Mitchell Visoky, Nancy Woogen, Kerry Yankowich, Ilga Zieimins-Kurens

Special thanks to: Miriam Arroyo, Barbara Bortle, Ellen Brooks, Angela Butler, Pat Conques, Dotti Griffin, Anahid Hamparian, Peggy Hansen, Sandy Harvilchuck, Naomi Hill, Carol Ann Jason, Jennifer Lombardo, Mary Lynne Oresen, Joanne Padow, Carol Patterson, Theresa Prairie, Tracy Racicot, Ellen Ramey, Linda Roy, Nicole Sawotka, Jude Smith, Faye Spielberger, Bev Strong, John Szakmary, Glen White, Mary Ellen Whitely

Benchmark Books
Marshall Cavendish
99 White Plains Road
Tarrytown, NY 10591-9001
www.marshallcavendish.com

Text copyright © 2003 by Jacqueline Sweeney
Illustrations copyright © 2003 by Marshall Cavendish Corporation

Book design by Anahid Hamparian

All rights reserved. No part of this book may be reproduced in any form without written permission of the publisher.
Library of Congress Cataloging-in-Publication Data
Poems about anger by America's children / edited by Jacqueline Sweeney.
  p. cm. -- (Kids express)
Summary: A collection of poetry and art by children describing their feelings about anger.
ISBN 0-7614-1508-4
1. Anger--Juvenile poetry. 2. Children's poetry, American. 3. Children's writings, American. [1. Anger--Poetry. 2. American poetry. 3. Children's writings. 4. Children's art.] I. Sweeney, Jacqueline. II. Series.
PS595.A48 P64 2002
811.008'0353--dc21
                    2002002707

Printed in Hong Kong
6 5 4 3 2 1

Carter Kelly, grade 3

Contents

Teacher's Note	4
I Am Mad	5
Punch What You Say	6
When Madness Was Going . . .	7
Angry	7
My Sock Smells So Bad	8
Eating Dinner	8
Don't Be Mean!	9
Red Hot!	10
When I'm mad	12
Crunch Monster	12
The Bitter Feeling of Mad . . .	13
Mad	14
Flower Quilt	15
Power!	16
The Cheetah Bear	17
I Am Really Hot	20
WHAT'S WITH THIS!	22
How Wonderful!	23
My Relieful Driveway	24
The Rip	24
My special place is the tree	25
Green Shutters	26
When I am mad my sister	28
A Magical Place	29
Art credits	30
Author index	31
Stop! Stop! Stop!	32

Teacher's Note

Imagine a classroom full of elementary school children bursting into applause upon hearing an announcement of an upcoming activity. Recess? Lunch? No. Writing poetry! Year after year, this is Jackie Sweeney's effect on students. I have been fortunate enough to witness this phenomenon over the last six years, as Jackie has conducted poetry residencies in the Arlington Central School District.

I study her as she teaches, trying to analyze her strategies. Although I have learned a lot from doing so, there is also some kind of magic at work here. Jackie is a modern-day alchemist, helping students turn their writing into something quite extraordinary.

What does she do? First, she convinces students that they are safe and their ideas are exciting. She focuses on free verse, providing structures through which she introduces students to poetic techniques such as sensory imagery, simile, metaphor, personification, and diction. At the same time, she invites students to surprise her with their own interpretations of these structures. She models extensively with examples from her own imagination and from the work of other students. Her samples are carefully chosen to counteract the notion that poetry treats only butterfly wings and flowers; topics range over every possible subject, from slithering pythons to pestering siblings.

Sensory perceptions are combined in surprising ways. Jackie might begin by asking students to picture a certain color and let it make them feel cold or hot or cool or warm. This is quickly developed into simile as she asks the students to consider how the color (let's say "red") is hot "like what?" As the students come up with their first tentative similes, Jackie immediately gets them to elaborate by asking questions until the child has produced: "Red makes me feel hot like a tomato on a white plate on a picnic table with the sun beating down on it on a summer day." Jackie exclaims, "Now I can see it!" and we are off on another year's excursion into poetry.

Peggy C. Hansen
Noxon Road Elementary School
Poughkeepsie, New York

I Am Mad

I'm mad at my brother I'm mad at mom I'm mad at my father I'm mad at my dog. It looks like I'm going to explode in the sun.

—Casey Nelson Tompkins, *grade 3*

—Chris Kiel, *grade 4*

Punch What You Say

You make the beast and then I let it out.

I punch what you say.

You think I'm your punching bag.

I think you're that little ignorant gremlin

hanging on my ear. And I blow you away.

I'm stuck in your web.

And you wrap me in your meanness.

I don't listen and break

free.

Now you're not real to me.

—Kienan Lynch, grade 3

—Rachael Lewis-Krisky, grade 4

When Madness Was Going Through My Veins

In first grade I didn't know how to tie my shoes. And my sisters were making fun of me. I felt like madness was going through my veins. It feels like a lion was biting me.

—Derrick Burleski, *grade 2*

Angry

I felt angry when my sister broke my new car that I got for Christmas. I felt so angry I wanted to flush something of hers down the toilet. My face was so red. I wish I could take her favorite toy and cut it in half. I wish I could take one of her toys and throw it in the trash. Finally I took one of her barbies and dunked its head in the toilet water.

—John Musumeci, *grade 3*

—Sarah Grange, *grade 6*

My Sock Smells So Bad

The smelliest thing is my sock after
soccer practice or hockey practice.
It smells like the fridge when my
brother puts his rotten banana in.
I don't like my brother. He's
usually asleep when I get home
so I stick my socks in his bed.
When I get home I take a shower
and my feet smell so bad I
hold my breath. I'm so sweaty
my socks stick to my feet.
Someday I wish I won't
have such smelly feet.

—Taylor, *grade 3*

Eating Dinner

My dog chases me around
and my mom says "stop
it, please."
Then at dinner time we
eat peas that look like rotten
watermelons and are red.
My dad says if I don't
eat them I will have to
go to bed.

—Dustin Decker, *grade 3*

Don't Be Mean!

I am mad because all the kids make fun of my name. I love my name. It is "Autumn." And sometimes they call me "Fall."

Do people call you names? I want to tell the boys to stop calling me names. I'm going to do a good thing today:

STOP CALLING ME NAMES! O.K.!

—Autumn Meyer grade 3

—Alyssa Dunlop, grade 4

Red Hot!

I'm so mad at this kid
I don't like. I
feel like making
him get blown up and
I won't care. I want
him to stay away
from me for the
rest of my life. I
hate him so much
I wish he went in
a rocket ship
and blasted off into
space and landed
on Uranus and he
got frozen stiff and
forever.

I hate this kid
because he said
that I like Barney
and other stuff like
that.

—Steven Chabot, *grade 3*

—Chris, *grade 6*

When I'm mad
I feel like a bookcase
then I yell and yell and
yell and yell and I throw
a fit and I run around
and I boss people around.

—Jocelynne Shepard, grade 1

Crunch Monster

When I'm mad
I feel like a monster
who's going to
crunch his body in the wall

—Jared Warren, grade 1

—Andrew Costa, grade 3

The Bitter Feeling of Mad and Loneliness

Being mad feels like a bitter apple
crawling through my taste buds.
It squeezes my heart and my brain until
I just can't take it anymore.
I try to hold it in but it swarms through
my body. When it shoves me too hard
with its punching and scratching
it just comes out.
Now someone is mad at me.
They think I was mad at them and
now it's the opposite.

I feel lonely like I have no friends.
My anger and fury has gone away.
But now someone else caught it
and I can't feel my heart because I'm depressed.
It doesn't help being mad.
It doesn't help to hold it in.
Just make sure that it doesn't roll onto
someone else's tongue.

—Sarah Apple, *grade 5*

Mad

The most maddest thing is
when my friends leave me out. They
pretend that I'm not there. I feel as
mad as a bucket of water with steam—
as mad as a person who can't find a word
in the dictionary. I could run over and hit
them on the head with a bat, and when they
wake up I'll hope they'll remember that
they forgot me. I am so mad I could go
clap dirty erasers in their faces!
I can feel my eyes popping out of my head!
It tastes like chalk that has been rolled
in mud. I could dress up like their
teacher and say: "one of the most
important things is not ignoring
your friends!" If they don't go
and say sorry or remember what they
forgot, I'll hit them on the head
with a bat again and wrap them
up in toilet paper, put them in a
wagon and roll them down a hill
and then put them in a giant wheel
and let them float in a pond with
snapping turtles and then hit them
with a book and send them
to the zoo! I want to send them
to the zoo because I want them to
live with the monkeys!

—Kate Wesley, *grade 3*

Flower Quilt

My special place is my little bedroom. I go there when my older and little brothers get on the same team of fighting at me. And they always win.

My little bedroom has a flower quilt, a silver blow up chair, a cute little white desk where I think of decisions that are hard to make.

I always lock the door so my brothers don't fight with me anymore.

I turn on my radio and crack it to the lowest volume. It is like a mouse squeaking in your ear.

I hear my brothers screaming at me, telling me to open the door.

Then I remember that they don't like any of my CDs. So then I turn on one of my CDs and crank it up louder than I ever did. And they run.

—Casey Benson, grade 4

—Jim Garay, grade 5

Power!

I am fierce and I don't let anybody push me around. When I get scared, the grizzly bear in me gives me faith and courage. He tells me to stand up to my fears. But when I'm not scared he is calm like a gentle breeze on summer day. He lives in my soul and is brave. He is strong with a will of steel. When I play soccer he is a brick wall. When I play football he gives me speed and power. But I guess he doesn't help me in basketball because I STINK. He is all my strength. Sometimes he comes into me out of nowhere and gives me the power to stand up to bullies. Yet he is calm when I'm bored. I think he's asleep. So that's why I don't do anything fun when I'm bored.

—Tyler Izykowski, *grade 5*

—Mike Hagan-Smith, *grade 3*

The Cheetah Bear

A cheetah is inside of me and I like when I feel him and I have brown eyes and blond hair and I can swim good. And I have a bear in my brain and he helps me beat bullies and now they are afraid of me. But I don't hurt them. I just scare them.

—Brandon Merlino, *grade 2*

—Peter Keenan, *grade 3*

—Jordan Thomson, *grade 4*

—Tara McNeill, *grade 4*

—Elizabeth Ahearn, *grade 4*

—Stephen Dowd, *grade 4*

I Am Really Hot

Yesterday I was really mad at
my little brother. When I
was standing up
watching T.V. he pushed
me down.
I got so mad thunder sounds
like my three screams.
I was so mad I screamed and
the whole house shook.

—Jessica Dominguez, *grade 2*

—Daniel Blayney, *grade 2*

WHAT'S WITH THIS!

Ballet! Soft music! This is
no place for me! I belong
where there's noise and contact
with helmets, bashing refs,
yelling coaches, arguing whistles
and horns going off, flags
being thrown, fouls being
called. People getting hit and
hurt. But right now I'm stuck
here with no contact and
no noise. Sometimes during
my sister's ballet I just want
to jump up and say
  WHAT'S WITH THIS!

—John Ortolano, *Grade 5*

How Wonderful!

The most wonderful thing
in the world is being alone.
When my big brother gets
through with me it's the
only thing I can think of.
It's purple like the soft
petals on flowers being
brushed by the wind.
Sometimes when I'm alone
I want my bestest bestest
friend Allyson to be right
there so we can play.
I wish I could make up
my mind.

—Julia Hopson, *grade 4*

—anonymous, *grade 4*

My Relieful Driveway

My favorite place is my driveway when I'm mad. I have to walk all of my anger out. If it is late enough I can see God's painting. I can hear all of the creatures—frogs and crickets. My driveway is about 400 feet long so all the anger gets out. Sometimes I get tired so I sit and think about what my parents are going to say. This is my anger relief place.

—Tiffany Peloquin, grade 5

The Rip

When I am sad I feel like a boy that dropped his bike on the ground. He is so sad because his friend called a mad word to him. I feel sad like a boy's kite that got stuck in a tree and it got a big rip in it. He told his dad. His dad made another kite for him.

—Cobi Adrian, grade 1

Marielle Rayer, grade 2

My special place is the tree in my front yard. I call it the Inner Circle. In the winter there's a rock in front of the tree and it is part of the Inner Circle. The rock and the tree are special to me because me and my mom sat on that rock the first year I was here and ate lunch. I go to it in spring and summer when my mom and dad are fighting or when I can't have my way. I go there when I'm lonely. When I look at the tree I kind of see family and friends.

—Samantha Calogero, grade 3

—Anthony Terilli, grade 2

Green Shutters

My secret place is in the closet.
I go there to hide when I'm upset
or angry. I also think I'm a spy.
I shine my flashlight on the
dark dark walls. I have the
key and I lock myself in 'til
I work things over.

In the summer I take my pillow,
sleeping bag and stuffed animals.
I tie my flashlight around the broken
light string. In storms I hear
my great green shutters
banging against the house.

I feel safe in the dark like
I'm in a cell, a very tiny cell
with walls of white. I feel like
I'm in the sky. I just lie there
floating. That closet is a
real special place.

—Stephanie Murray, *grade 3*

—Veronica Jones, *grade 3*

—Abby Reisner, *grade 4*

When I am mad my sister gives me her musical stuffed unicorn. When the world stops it is calm.

—Heather Knapp, *grade 2*

—Madeleine Ouellette, grade 5

A Magical Place

My special place is in the woods.
It's a whole different world.
I pretend it's a laboratory and I'm a
scientist trying to figure out a way
for happiness. In my fort everything's
possible.

—George Griffeth, *grade 3*

—Glenna Nickerson, *grade 5*

—Ian Arturo, *grade 5*

Art credits

Daniel Blayney cover, 21

Mike Hagan-Smith title page, 16

Carter Kelly copyright page

Chris Kiel 5, back cover

Rachael Lewis-Krisky 6

Sarah Grange 7, back cover

Alyssa Dunlop 9

Chris 11

Andrew Costa 12, back cover

Jim Garay 15

Peter Keenan 17

Jordan Thomson 18 (top)

Tara McNeill 18 (bottom)

Elizabeth Ahearn 19 (top)

Stephen Dowd 19 (bottom)

Anonymous 23

Marielle Rayer 24

Anthony Terilli 25

Veronica Jones 27 (top)

Abby Reisner 27 (bottom)

Madeleine Ouellette 28

Glenna Nickerson 29 (top)

Ian Arturo 29 (bottom)

Author index

Adrian, Cobi 24

Apple, Sarah 13

Benson, Casey 15

Burleski, Derrick 7

Calogero, Samantha 25

Chabot, Steven 10

Decker, Dustin 8

Dominguez, Jessica 20

Griffeth, George 29

Hopson, Julia 23

Izykowski, Tyler 16

Knapp, Heather 28

Lynch, Kienan 6

Merlino, Brandon 17

Meyer, Autumn 9

Murray, Stephanie 26

Musumeci, John 7

Ortolano, John 22

Peloquin, Tiffany 24

Schaut, Kaitlyn 32

Shepard, Jocelynne 12

Taylor 8

Tompkins, Casey Nelson 5

Warren, Jared 12

Wesley, Kate 14

—Kaitlyn Schaut, grade 3

RISING SUN
ELEMENTARY SCHOOL
MEDIA CENTER